Anonymous

The Burlington Fine Arts Club

Anonymous

The Burlington Fine Arts Club

ISBN/EAN: 9783744666428

Printed in Europe, USA, Canada, Australia, Japan

Cover: Foto ©ninafisch / pixelio.de

More available books at **www.hansebooks.com**

THE

Burlington Fine Arts Club,

17, SAVILE ROW, W.

RULES, REGULATIONS, AND BYE-LAWS,

WITH

LIST OF MEMBERS.

1899.

CONTENTS.

GENERAL NOTICES.

Entrance Fee and Subscription.

The Entrance Fee is £5 5s., payable on Election, and the Annual Subscription is £5 5s., payable also on Election, and thenceforth on 1st January in each year (Rule XIX.).

Bankers.

The London and Westminster Bank (St. James's Square Branch) are appointed Bankers, to whom Members now, or hereafter to be, admitted, are required to pay their several Subscriptions.

To avoid inconvenience, and to ensure punctual payment, it is requested that Members will furnish their Bankers or Agents with authority to pay the Annual Subscription on 1st January.

Library.

Members of the Club are invited to present copies of their published or privately printed works, or any other useful Art publications, especially books of reference, to the Library.

They are also invited to contribute, by Annual Subscription, to the Library Fund.

The Burlington Fine Arts Club.

COMMITTEE FOR 1898–99.

BENSON, ROBERT H., *Trustee*
BROS, J. R. W.
BROWNLOW, THE EARL
CARMICHAEL, SIR T. GIBSON, BT., M.P.
DILLON, EDWARD
MILLS, RICHARD, *Trustee*
MONKHOUSE, W. COSMO
POYNTER, SIR EDWARD J., P.R.A.
RATE, LACHLAN MACKINTOSH
RAWLINSON, W. G.
ROGET, JOHN L.
TEBBS, H. VIRTUE } *Trustees*
VAUGHAN, HENRY
WEDMORE, FREDERICK
WINDSOR, RT. HON. THE LORD

BANKERS.

LONDON AND WESTMINSTER BANK,
St. James's Square.

History of the Club.

T HE BURLINGTON FINE ARTS CLUB may be considered as the successor and representative of two distinct bodies, the one a party of friends interested in Art, and particularly in Engraved Prints and Drawings, amongst whom were the late Mr. Felix Slade (the generous donor of so many Fine Art objects to the British Museum, and the Founder of the several Fine Art Professorships which preserve the memory of his name), Sir Charles Price, Mr. Richard Fisher, and Sir Wollaston Franks, who, about the middle of this century, were in the habit of meeting together, in an inner room at Messrs. Graves's, in Pall Mall, a somewhat similar gathering taking place at a subsequent period at the house of Mr. Toovey, in Piccadilly. The other body was the " Fine Arts Club," founded in 1857, " for the " object of facilitating intercourse between men " of Art predilections, and especially those who " were collectors, with a view of giving to them " convenient opportunities of comparing their " acquisitions, and of criticising and obtaining " information in connection with Art subjects."

This Club comprised most if not all of the same circle, who, with many others, used to hold social gatherings on several evenings during the London season at each other's houses in turn, and charming receptions were given at some of the principal houses in London when collections of Works of Art and Vertu were brought together for exhibition. This was at a time when Club houses, now so numerous, were few, and there was none specially dedicated to Art and its Collectors, and also before the foundation of the South Kensington Museum, or when it was only in the early years of its existence. At this time, also, the collections at the British Museum were far less extensive than at present. With the exception of the gatherings occasionally held at the Royal Society of Antiquaries, this social society gave at the time to those interested in the Fine Arts almost the only opportunities of showing and comparing their collections.

The survivors of those who were thus privileged to attend will recall with pleasure and gratitude the memorable evenings spent at the house of Mr. John Malcolm, of Poltalloch, when his splendid collection of drawings by the Old Masters were so well shown; the rich and varied collections of Mr. John Henderson, of Mr. Holford, Mr. Marjoribanks, Mr. Beresford-Hope, Baron Marochetti, Lord Overstone, Mr. Gladstone and others: Mr. Robinson (now Sir Charles Robinson) being the first Honorary Secretary and chief organiser.

It will be remembered that the Exhibition at Manchester in 1857 was the first formed solely to show the Fine Arts as such, whilst the first important Collection of Works of Art on loan at South Kensington was held in 1862.

However, towards the end of the year 1866, the gatherings of the before-mentioned friends at Mr. Toovey's had become too numerous for convenience, and it was resolved to form a Club where they and others could meet as heretofore, but on their own premises. The upper part of Mr. Toovey's house, No. 177, Piccadilly, was then taken, and a Club was formed in December, 1866, limited to 250 members, of which the Marquis d'Azeglio, then Sardinian Minister in London, was elected Chairman, and it was joined by most of the members of the "Fine Arts Club." But the latter still continued for a few years to exist as a separate body.

The new Club took the name of the Burlington Fine Arts Club from its position opposite

Burlington House, to which the Royal Academy had recently moved. The limiting number of the Club has since been extended to 500.

A prospectus was issued stating that—

" Several gentlemen, amateurs and collectors " of Works of Art, having from time to time " conversed on the subject of the formation of a " Club or Society for the furtherance of know- " ledge of Art, and for social intercourse in " general, have constituted themselves into a " Society for that purpose.

" The want of any suitable place of meeting " for persons of kindred tastes in Art has long " been felt, and it is thought that the increasing " number of gentlemen who are more or less " devoted to artistic pursuits has now brought " the formation of a special Art Club within the " sphere of possibility.

" With all true amateurs the pleasure arising " from the possession of Works of Art is enhanced " by the interest and appreciation which they " excite in others, whilst at the same time instruc- " tion and refinement of taste can only result in " their fullest measure from frequent communica- " tion with persons possessing special knowledge " in the several branches of Art.

" Hitherto, however, the opportunities for such

" general social intercourse have been very few,
" and nothing like a general aggregation of
" artistic society has as yet been formed in
" London."

Later papers issued by the Club define its
objects to be, in brief, to bring together, on a
friendly footing, collectors, amateurs and persons
variously interested in matters of Art, and to
provide a centre for the exhibition and com-
parison among its Members of objects of interest
in their possession. Secondly, to utilise these
Exhibitions by making them from time to time
subservient to the illustration of particular arts,
or the art of a particular master or period, and
to render them under certain restrictions acces-
sible to a portion of the public.

There were held in these rooms at Piccadilly
several Exhibitions of much interest. First, of
Etchings chiefly of the French school, followed
by a series of three Exhibitions, designed to
illustrate the special modes of working of the
Dutch, Italian, and German schools, viz., in 1867,
a collection of the Engraved Work of Rembrandt,
in which was included every copy of the so-called
" hundred guilder " print, then and now of
the greatest rarity, which was in private hands.
It should be stated that this was distinct from

the magnificent collection subsequently shown in Savile Row in 1877. Then in 1868 "the "Engraved Copies and Adaptations of Marc "Antonio and his contemporaries," followed, in 1869, by the Engravings, Woodcuts and Drawings of Albert Durer and Lucas van Leiden. There was held earlier in the same year a collection of Oriental Art especially rich in Jade and Porcelain.

The last Exhibition held in the Piccadilly rooms was in 1870, and consisted of original Drawings by Raphael and Michael Angelo, with some Engravings and Photographs from works by those artists, principally of designs and compositions which have been lost, and of which no other record is extant.

At this time the British Institution, which for many years had held Exhibitions of the works of the Old Masters in Painting, had somewhat fallen into decay, and the lease of the premises occupied by it in Pall Mall was about to expire, and could not be renewed. It was therefore proposed by the Committee of the Burlington Club that the Club should undertake for the future this important task in their place, and for this purpose the Club was ready to build a suitable Gallery.

Negotiations were opened with the Directors and Trustees of the British Institution, who, subject to certain conditions, were prepared to assent to this course, and if it were found practicable, to hand over for this purpose, the large funds which had accumulated in their hands, to the younger body. The then President of the Royal Academy, Sir Francis Grant, was also favourable to the plan, and the necessary arrangements were almost completed when some other Members of the Royal Academy considered that the work of holding such Exhibitions of the works of the older Masters could be better carried out by the Academy itself, as a public body, in their own Galleries during the winter months, and this has fortunately been done with brilliant success and with the greatest usefulness, as will be in the recollection of all interested in Fine Art. But it is perhaps worth putting thus on record that the first conception and initial scheme for this was the work of the Burlington Club, though its realisation by the Royal Academy has been far more important than it could have been in the hands of a private institution. .   .

In the year 1870 the Club moved to their present premises in Savile Row, where they built the Gallery which has been the scene of so many interesting collections. The funds necessary for that purpose and for furnishing the Club were raised by Members, who subscribed £4,500 on Debentures, of which £2,375 has been paid off out of Entrance Fees which are set aside for the purpose. Amongst the Exhibitions of special interest may be mentioned the fine collection made in 1872, when there was for the first time a complete Exhibition of Turner's Liber Studiorum, a great boon to collectors and others interested in this his noblest work, followed up in later years by several smaller Exhibitions of special subjects from the Liber series, in which the unique engraver's proofs, from the rich collections of Mr. J. E. Taylor, Mr. Henry Vaughan and Mr. Rawlinson, were shown together. The more complete Exhibition in 1877 of the Etched work of Rembrandt, arranged and described by Sir Seymour Haden and the Rev. C. H. Middleton, now the Rev. C. H. Middleton-Wake. The pictures of George Mason and Dante Gabriel Rossetti were also shown here after the death of these artists, the latter Exhibition being attended by 12,133 visitors. The noble collections of Portrait Miniatures and of Bookbindings will also be in the memory of the Members of the Club and its visitors.

A complete list of the Exhibitions held will be found at pp. 21–24.

Of some of the earlier Exhibitions held at Piccadilly no Catalogue was prepared, but Catalogues were issued in 1868 and 1869. From the year 1870 these have been regularly issued to the Members, and form interesting monographs which are much valued.

Enlarged editions of the following Catalogues, with Illustrations, have also been issued to the special subscribers—

English and Continental Porcelain, 1873.

Bronzes and Ivories of European Origin, 1879.

Persian and Arab Art, 1885.

Greek Ceramic Art, 1888.

Portrait Miniatures, 1889.

Bookbindings, 1891.

Early Netherlandish Pictures, 1892.

Ferrara-Bologna School, 1894.

European Enamels, 1897.

Milanese School, 1898.

In addition, Addresses have occasionally been given and Papers read at the Club evenings, as, for instance, by Professor Maskelyne on Jade and its Allies, 14th April, 1876, and on Greek

Coins, with illustrations, and a long series of Originals and Electrotypes, by Mr. H. Virtue Tebbs, in November, 1874.

In the year 1874, the old " Fine Arts Club " came to an end in the following manner :—

A Special Meeting was held on the 13th March, 1874, with Sir William Drake in the Chair, when the following notice, which had been previously sent to each Member, was placed upon the table as read :—

" *2nd March*, 1874.

· " I am directed to inform you that at a meeting of the Committee of the Fine Arts Club, held on the 26th January last, the following resolution, confirmed at a subsequent meeting of the Committee, held on the 26th February, was passed :—

" That in the opinion of this Committee, the objects " for which this Club was established in 1856 " have been fulfilled, and that the time has now " arrived when the further continuance of the " Association will not effectually aid in the " accomplishment of its purpose, and that steps " be taken to ascertain the views of the Mem- " bers generally on the point, for which purpose " a General Meeting of the Club be called at as " early a date as practicable."

" I am now instructed to invite your attendance at a General Meeting of the Club, to be held at

the house of the Burlington Fine Arts Club,
17, Savile Row, on Friday, the 13th instant, at
four o'clock precisely, when the above resolution
will be submitted; and in the event of its meeting
with the concurrence of the Members present,
resolutions will be proposed as to the disposal
of the funds in hand belonging to the Club.

I am, &c.,

W. MATCHWICK,

Acting Secretary."

The Chairman, after recalling the earlier
history of the Club, stated that the gatherings of
the Association were in its early stage more
distinctly limited to the object for which it was
founded; but by degrees the social element
prevailed, and meetings were held and charming
receptions were given at the principal houses in
London, when collections of Works of Art were
brought together for exhibition. It was about
this time (1866) that several of the leading
Members of the Club felt that an association of
a less peripatetic character, having a local habi-
tation as well as a name, and embracing in its
objects similar purposes to those of this Club,
should be formed; and accordingly the Burlington Fine Arts Club was established.

After some other remarks on the old Club, the Chairman concluded by moving the following resolution, which was duly seconded by Mr. Fisher:—

> "That the opinion of the Committee, as expressed "in their resolution of the 26th January, now "read, is concurred in by this meeting, and it is "therefore resolved that, subject to the adjust-"ment by the Committee of the debts and "liabilities of the Association, this Club be and "the same is dissolved."

Some observations and discussion followed, and the resolution was put to the meeting and carried *nem. con.*

The Chairman then moved the following resolution, which was seconded by Mr. Henderson :—

> "That the Committee are authorised and empowered "to distribute the funds of the Club, which may "remain in the hands of the Treasurer, after "payment of all debts and liabilities, in such "manner as to them may seem expedient and "proper."

The resolution was put to the meeting and carried unanimously.

The Chairman then declared, pursuant to the resolution which had been passed by the meeting, that the Fine Arts Club was dissolved ; and thanks being given to him for his conduct in the Chair, the meeting separated.

On the dissolution of this older Club the funds remaining in the hands of its Trustees were handed over to the Burlington Club for the purchase of books relating to the Fine Arts, which became the nucleus of the present Library, since so much increased by the generous gifts and the subscriptions of Members. It now comprises several thousand volumes, and is yearly increasing.

On the resignation of the Marquis d'Azeglio, Sir William Drake was chosen Chairman, and so continued until his death in 1890. His able management greatly contributed to the success of the Club. He was succeeded by the Earl of Strafford and afterwards by the Earl Brownlow.

A list of the Members of the Club in 1899 is given on page 43.

H. V. T,

Special Exhibitions held at the Club.

1867
{ Etchings. Chiefly of the French School.
{ Etchings and Engravings by Rembrandt.

1868
{ Engravings by Marc Antonio Raimondi.
{ Oriental Porcelain.

1869
{ Engravings by Albert Dürer and Lucas van Leyden.
{ Oriental Art.

1870
{ Original Drawings by Raphael Sanzio and Michel Angelo Buonarroti.

1871
{ Pictures by Old Masters.
{ Drawings in Water Colours by deceased English Artists, born anterior to 1800.

1872
{ Turner's Liber Studiorum.
{ Drawings and Etchings by Claude.
{ Drawings by William Müller.
{ Pictures by George Mason, A.R.A.

1873
{ English and Continental Porcelain.
{ Drawings and Sketches by David Cox and Peter de Wint.

1874
{ Illuminated Manuscripts.
{ Greek Coins.

1875	Selection from the work of Wenceslaus Hollar. The works of Thomas Girtin. Japanese Lacquer Ware.
1876	Artistic Painted Glass. The works of William Blake.
1877	The Etched Work of Rembrandt. The works of Hans Sebald Beham and Barthel Beham.
1878	Collected works of John Samuel Raven. Drawings by Dutch Masters. Japanese and Chinese Works of Art.
1879	Bronzes and Ivories of European Origin. Selection from the work of Charles Méryon.
1880	Drawings in Water Colours by deceased English Artists, born subsequent to 1800.
1881	Engravings in Mezzotinto.
1882	Woodcuts of the German School of the Fifteenth and Sixteenth Centuries.
1883	Pictures and Drawings by Dante Gabriel Rossetti. Etchings by Renier Zeeman and Karel Du Jardin.
1884	Drawings of Architectural Subjects by deceased British Artists.

1885   Persian and Arab Art.

1886 {
The works of James McArdell.
Some of Turner's Liber Studiorum Plates.
Illuminations from French MSS.

1887   Hispano-Moresque and Majolica Pottery.

1888 {
Japanese Engraving.
Greek Ceramic Art.
Drawings by John Sell Cotman.

1889   Portrait Miniatures.

1890   Drawings by Spencer Vincent.

1891 {
French Revival of Etching.
Bookbindings.

1892 {
Pictures by Masters of the Netherlandish and
allied Schools of the XV. and early XVI.
Centuries.

1893   The work of Luca Signorelli and his School.

1894 {
Japanese Lacquer and Metal Work.
Works by Masters of the School of Ferrara-
Bologna.

1895 {
Blue and White Oriental Porcelain.
Art of Ancient Egypt.

1896   Coloured Chinese Porcelain.

1897 {
Drawings by Alfred William Hunt, R.W.S.
European Enamels.

1898 { Pictures by Masters of the Milanese and allied
       Schools of Lombardy.

1899 { Drawings and Studies of Sir Edward Burne-
       Jones, Bart.

N.B.—*Surplus Copies of the Catalogues of the above Exhibitions, with a few exceptions, still remain (including some Illustrated Editions), and may be obtained, by Members of the Club only, at prices which can be ascertained on application to the Secretary, Mr. John Beavan.*

Objects of the Club.

The constitution and purpose of the BURLING-
TON FINE ARTS CLUB may be stated in brief to
be—

I.—To bring together Amateurs, Collectors,
and others interested in Art; to afford ready
means for consultation between persons of
special knowledge and experience in matters
relating to the Fine Arts; and to provide
accommodation for showing and comparing rare
works in the possession of the Members and
their friends.

II.—To provide in the Reading Room (in
addition to usual newspapers) periodicals, books,
and catalogues, foreign as well as English, having
reference to Art, it being the intention to render
the Club a means of obtaining knowledge of all
sales or other opportunities for the acquisition of
Works of Art; and to make it a general medium
of information on points relating to the history
and condition of the Fine Arts both at home
and abroad.

III.—To make arrangements in the Gallery
and Rooms of the Club for the exhibition of

pictures, original drawings, engravings, and rare books, enamels, ceramic wares, coins, plate, and other valuable works.

IV.—To hold, in addition to the above, once in the year or oftener, Special Exhibitions which shall have for their object the elucidation of some School, Master, or specific Art. Members to have the privilege of introducing friends to these special collections.

V.—To render the Club a centre where occasionally, especially when works of more than usual interest are on view, Conversazioni may be held of an Art character. Members to have the power of introducing two visitors, ladies or gentlemen.

VI.—To provide, in addition to the above Art objects, the ordinary accommodation and advantages of a London Club, including Reading, News, Billiard and Smoking Rooms; and to provide House Dinners and Refreshments on such a scale as may be found practicable.

The Club possesses a valuable Library of Books of Reference on Art, to which additions are constantly being made by means of a Library Fund.

RULES AND REGULATIONS.

1899.

THE

Burlington Fine Arts Club.

RULES AND REGULATIONS.

I.

HE CLUB is formed for the purpose Objects of the Club. of bringing together in social intercourse Amateurs, Collectors, and others interested in Art, and affording them a ready means of inter-communication on matters connected with the Fine Arts, and facilitating the Exhibition of acquisitions made from time to time by its Members or their friends.

2. The Club to consist of not more than Number of Members. Five Hundred Members, exclusive of Honorary Members.

3. The general and pecuniary management Management. and direction of the concerns of the Club, including the appointment and removal of all Officers and Servants, is vested in a Committee to be composed of not less than Twelve Members.

Powers of
Committee.

4. The Committee to regulate their mode of procedure, and to meet at such times as they may consider necessary for the transaction of business. They have power from time to time to make and rescind such Bye-laws (not inconsistent with these Rules) as may in their judgment be proper for the regulation of the affairs of the Club; such Bye-laws to be printed and placed in the Morning Room. The quorum of the Committee for ordinary business is Three; but for the purposes of election of Members the quorum is Five. All matters (except the election of Members) not unanimously agreed on by the Committee, are to be decided by the votes of a majority of the Members present.

Election of
Committee.

5. The Committee is to be elected by Balloting Lists at the Annual General Meeting of the Club in May, one-third of the existing Committee retiring annually by rotation; such retiring Members being, however, eligible for re-election.

Retiring
Members of
Committee.

6. Ten clear days before the Annual General Meeting a list of the names of the Members of the Committee retiring by rotation is to be placed in the Morning Room, and the notice is to specify the retiring Members who offer themselves for re-election.

7. Six clear days' notice, previous to the Annual General Meeting, is to be given by letter addressed to the Committee, of the names of any gentleman (other than a retiring Member) intended to be proposed as a Member of the Committee, and the notice so given is to be placed in the Morning Room. Without such notice no new name can be proposed.

8. In the event of any Vacancies occurring in the Committee after the annual election, the Committee have the power of filling such Vacancies; but the gentlemen so elected by the Committee shall be included in the number retiring at the General Meeting following their election.

9. The election of Members of the Club is vested in the Committee, and is to be by ballot; two black balls to exclude.

10. The name and address of every Candidate for admission as a Member of the Club must be entered in the Candidates' Book, and the entry signed by a proposer and seconder, or by authority received from them. Members desirous of supporting the election may affix their signatures to the entry.

11. Names of Candidates, with those of their proposers and seconders, to be suspended in

Morning Room. the Morning Room of the Club a fortnight before the dates of election.

Exceptional Elections by Committee. 12. The Committee has the power to elect as Members of the Club gentlemen holding distinguished Art appointments in. Scotland, Ireland, or on the Continent, on payment of the Entrance Fee of £5 5s., and an Annual Subscription of £1 1s., such Annual Subscription, however, to be raised to £5 5s., in case such Members should become permanently resident in England.

Annual Meeting. 13. An Annual General Meeting of the Members of the Club to be held once a year on such day and hour in the month of May as the Committee may from time to time appoint.

Report and Accounts. 14. The Committee to submit to the Annual General Meeting the Accounts of the Club for the preceding year, with a report as to the general position of its affairs, together with an estimate of the expenditure for the ensuing year.

Special General Meetings. 15. It is competent for the Committee at any time to call Special General Meetings, and they are bound to do so on a requisition in writing signed by Ten Members of the Club, and specifying the object of such Meeting, the discussion at which shall be confined to that object.

16. A Special General Meeting may be called **Expulsion.** to consider the expediency of expelling any Member from the Club, and such Meeting shall have the power of expulsion on any grounds considered sufficient by two-thirds of the Members present thereat. Any person who may be expelled forfeits *ipso facto* all right to or claim, as a Member, upon the Club or its property or its funds.

17. The quorum for Special General Meetings **Quorum for Special General Meetings.** is Fifteen.

18. Six clear days' notice of all General Meet- **Notices of General Meetings.** ings to be given by circular posted to the address of each Member of the Club resident in Great Britain. In the case of a Special General Meeting the circular shall specify the object of the Meeting.

19. The Entrance Fee is £5 5*s.*, payable **Entrance Fee and Subscription.** on election, and the Annual Subscription is £5 5*s.*, payable also on election, and thenceforth on the 1st of January in each year.

20. If the new Member does not pay his **Payment of Entrance Fee and Subscription.** Entrance Fee and first Annual Subscription within three months from his election, the Committee shall, unless the non-payment be explained to their satisfaction, erase his name from the list of Members.

Defaulters.
21. The names of any Members failing to pay their Annual Subscription to be placed in the Morning Room on the 1st of February, and unless the Subscription be paid on or before the 1st of April following, such Members to cease from that time to belong to the Club, except a satisfactory explanation of the delay in payment be given to the Committee. To avoid inconvenience it is earnestly requested that Members will furnish their Bankers or Agents with authority to pay their Annual Subscriptions on 1st January.

Restrictions as to Works of living Artists.
22. The main object of the Club being the exhibition of Works of Art of past ages, the Works of living Artists will be admitted only upon special application from the Committee.

Works for exhibition.
23. Works for exhibition can only be admitted with the sanction of the Committee. No reason will be assigned for the exclusion of any object offered for exhibition.

Works for exhibition to be deposited at Members' own risk.
24. Objects of Art deposited by Members for exhibition in the rooms of the Club are to be so deposited entirely on their own risk and responsibility.

Duration of exhibition.
25. No object is to remain for exhibition for a longer period than one month, except at the special desire of the Committee.

26. Members have the privilege of personally Visitors. introducing Visitors, subject to the Bye-laws or Regulations of the Committee.

27. Exhibitions of Works of Art and Conver- Exhibitions and Conver- sazioni for artistic purposes may be held in the sazioni. Rooms of the Club, with the sanction and under the control and regulations of the Committee.

28. Except at Conversazioni, Exhibitions, or Visitors. Special Meetings, each Member may daily personally introduce not more than two friends, who will be admitted, while in his company, to all the privileges of the Club. The names of the Visitors, and of the Member introducing them, shall be entered by the latter in a book on their arrival. It is within the competency of the Committee from time to time, by Bye-law, to restrict, suspend, cancel, or enlarge this rule whenever in their opinion it is expedient to do so in the general interests of the Club.

29. At any Conversazione to be held at the Visitors at Conver- Club each Member may introduce personally sazioni. two friends (either ladies or gentlemen).

29A. In case of Special Exhibitions, Mem- Admission to Special bers may, subject to regulations to be from Exhibitions. time to time made by the Committee, introduce, personally or by ticket, a certain number of friends.

Foreign Honorary Members. 30. The Committee may, if they think fit, on the recommendation of two Members, admit Artists, eminent Collectors, Literary Men, and others distinguished in Art, residing permanently abroad, as Honorary Members of the Club (without admission-fee or subscription), such Honorary Members being admitted to the privileges of the Club during any temporary residence in England, or for such limited period as the Committee may fix.

Honorary Members. 31. Foreign Ambassadors and Ministers may be nominated by the Committee Honorary Members of the Club during their respective missions. Other members of the Diplomatic **Honorary Visitors.** Body accredited to the Court of St. James's may be invited by the Committee to attend personally the Club as Honorary Visitors for the space of three months: a renewal of these invitations being at the discretion of the Committee.

Privileges of Honorary Members and Visitors. 32. Honorary Members and Visitors to enjoy all the privileges of the Club, except that of introducing friends.

Opening and closing of Club-house. 33. The Club-house to be open every day from 10 o'clock A.M. to 12 P.M., when the outer door will be closed. Any Members, however, who may happen to be then within the house to be allowed to remain.

34. Any Member intending to be absent from the United Kingdom for one entire year or longer may, by giving notice to the Committee, be placed on the list of Supernumerary Members; and on his return he will be re-admitted, without ballot, as an ordinary Member of the Club, on payment of his full Subscription for the then current year.

35. All Members whilst on the Supernumerary List to pay an Annual Subscription of One Guinea only.

36. Any Member using the Club after the date on which his Subscription is due will be liable for the Subscription for the current year.

37. No Member shall take away, or permit to be taken away, from the Club, on any pretence whatever, or shall injure or destroy, any Newspaper or other article exhibited by or belonging to the Club. No paper, pamphlet, or books are to be introduced into the Club without the sanction of the Committee.

38. In case of Members wishing to have a house-dinner, a room may, with the consent of the Committee, be provided for that purpose, the Club having nothing whatever to do with either the providing the dinner or the service.

Gratuities. 39. No Member shall give any money or gratuity to the servants of the Club.

No accounts to be opened with Servants. 40. No account shall be opened by any Member of the Club with any of the servants.

Games of Chance. 41. No dice are to be used, and no Games of Chance are to be played in the Club.

Cards. 42. The charge for each pack of Cards will be 1s. 6d. by daylight, and 2s. by candlelight. Two candles are to be allowed for each table.

Dogs. 43. No dogs are to be admitted into the Club.

Alteration of Rules. 44. The Rules and Regulations for the time being of the Club may be altered or varied, but only at a Special General Meeting, and the proposed alterations or substitutions shall be fully specified in the Notice calling the meeting, and shall only be binding on the Club in the event of their being adopted by two-thirds of the Members then present.

Addresses of Members. 45. Each Member of the Club shall communicate his address to the Committee, and all notices posted to that address shall be considered as duly delivered.

Rules to be printed and furnished to Members. 46. Each Member shall be furnished with a printed copy of these Rules and Regulations; but no Member shall be absolved from the effect thereof on any allegation of not having received such printed copy.

BYE-LAWS

Made by the Committee under Rule 4.

6th February, 1872, *amended 2nd July,* 1895.

I. That the entry in the Candidates' Book shall state the Candidate's name and usual place of residence, his rank, profession, or other description, and the place where he exercises his profession or carries on his business.

That no Candidate can be balloted for unless a previous communication has been made in writing to the Committee, either by the Proposer or Seconder, certifying from *personal* knowledge that the Gentleman proposed will, from his social position, as well as from his cultivated taste, interest in Art, or other qualifications, be a desirable Member of the Burlington Fine Arts Club. No Dealer in Works of Art is eligible as a Candidate.

19th February, 1872.

II. That any Member of the Club may be at liberty to bring Works of Art, and leave them for a period not exceeding a fortnight in the Rooms on the second floor of the Club, for inspection and discussion.

23rd April, 1872.

III. That the creation of periodical vacancies in the Committee, so as to admit from time to time of new Members taking part in the management of the Club, is highly desirable, and with this view the Committee shall, previous to each Annual Meeting, propose to a majority only of the retiring Members to offer themselves for re-election.

22nd April, 1873.

IV. That no Member shall be entitled to assume, from the fact of the exhibition in the Rooms of the Club of any work of Art being his property, that the Club admits the authenticity or identity of the same.

15th December, 1874.

V. That the report of the General Committee in Manuscript, together with the Balance-sheet, also in Manuscript, for the preceding year, be laid on the table of the Reading Room at least one week before the day appointed for each Annual Meeting.

25th October, 1898.

VI. That with a view of giving additional facilities for the exhibition of works of Art in the Drawing Room, as provided by Rule 23, it shall be competent to any Two Members of the Committee, acting togther, to authorise objects offered on loan, which they may consider of sufficient merit and importance, to be exhibited in the Drawing Room, subject to the confirmation of the next meeting of the Committee; but this modification of the existing Bye-laws is not in any manner to affect the rights of the Members of the Club under Bye-law No. 2.

LIST OF MEMBERS,

FEBRUARY, 1899.

LIST OF MEMBERS,
1899.

ABDY, SIR W. NEVILLE, BART.

AINSLIE, DOUGLAS

ALDENHAM, THE LORD

ALEXANDER, WILLIAM C.

AMHERST OF HACKNEY, THE LORD

ANDERSON, ARCHIBALD

ANDERSON, PROFESSOR WILLIAM, F.R.C.S.

ARBUTHNOT, CHARLES GEORGE

ARCHDALE, GEORGE

ARMSTRONG, WALTER

ARTHUR, THOMAS GLEN

ASTON, WILLIAM WALLIS

AVERY, SAMUEL P.

BACON, SIR HICKMAN B., BART.

BACON, THOS. WALTER

BALCARRES, THE LORD

BALFOUR, EUSTACE J. A.

BATHURST, CHARLES

BEAUMONT, SOMERSET

BEHRENS, WALTER L.

BENCE-JONES, ARCHIBALD B.

Carysfort, The Earl of, K.P.
Cates, Arthur
Chadwyck-Healey, C. E. H., Q.C.
Chaplin, Holroyd
Cheylesmore, The Lord
Church, Professor A. H., F.R.S.
Clanrikarde, Marquis of
Clarke, Somers
Cohen, Alfred L.
Coles, Edward G.
Colvin, Professor Sidney
Cook, Sir Francis, Bart.
Cook, Herbert F.
Cope, W. H.
Corfield, W. H., M.D.
Cowper, The Earl, K.G.
Crawley, G. A.
Crews, Charles T. D.
Croft, George C.
Curzon, William
Cuvelje, Thomas
D'Arcy, W. Knox
Davenport, Cyril James
Davies, George R.
De Mauley, The Lord
Dent, Clinton T.
Devitt, Thomas L.

De Zoete, Walter M.

Dilke, Sir Charles W., Bart., M.P.

Dillon, Edward

Dillon, Frank

Dobree, Bonamy

Douglas, Greville

Drake, Lt.-Col. A. W. H. Hornsby-

Durning-Lawrence, Sir E., Bart., M.P.

Egerton of Tatton, The Earl

Erman, Professor, *Hon. Member*

Eumorfopoulos, George

Evans, Sir John, K.C.B., F.R.S.

Farrer, H. L.

Farrer, Sir William J.

Felton, W.

Fenwick, George

Field, J. Leslie

Field, Walter

Fisher, R. C.

Fleischmann, F.

Flower, Wickham

Forbes, James Staats

Forrest, George William

Fortnum, C. Drury E., D.C.L.

Fraser, Simon Henry

Freshfield, Douglas W.

Frizzoni, Dr. Gustavo, *Hon. Member*

FRÖHNER, DR. W., *Hon. Member*

FRY, LEWIS, M.P.

GARDNER, J. STARKIE

GASKELL, FRANCIS

GATHORNE-HARDY, HON. ALFRED E.

GIBBS, ANTONY

GILBERTSON, EDWARD

GODMAN, F. DU CANE

GOFF, COLONEL R.

GOLDMANN, CHARLES S.

GOLDSCHMIDT, ADOLPH B. H.

GORDON, HENRY EVANS

GOSSET, MAJ.-GEN. M. W. E., C.B.

GOWLAND, WILLIAM

GRAHAM, ALEXANDER

GREEN, EVERARD

GREENWOOD, HUBERT J.

HALLÉ, CHARLES E.

HARBEN, H. A.

HARDY, PAUL

HARLAND-PECK, G.

HARRIS, F. LEVERTON

HARRISON, LAWRENCE

HAY, HON. CLAUDE

HEAD, ALBAN

HENDERSON, ALEXANDER, M.P.

HERKOMER, PROFESSOR HUBERT, R. A.

HICHENS, ANDREW K.

HICHENS, REV. T. SIKES

HIGGINS, ALFRED

HILLINGDON, THE LORD

HILTON, JAMES

HOLFORD, CAPTAIN G. L., C.I.E.

HOLROYD, CHARLES

HOLZMANN, MAURICE, C.B.

HORNE, HERBERT P.

HUTH, EDWARD

HUTH, LOUIS

HYMANS, HENRI, *Hon. Member*

INGELOW, BENJAMIN

INMAN, THOMAS FREDERICK

IONIDES, CONSTANTINE A.

JACKSON, T. W.

JAMES, ARTHUR JOHN

JAMES, FRANCIS EDWARD

JAMES, WILLIAM D.

JARVIS, LEWIS

JEKYLL, LT.-COL. HERBERT, C.M.G.

JEX-BLAKE, VERY REV. T. W., D.D.

KAHN, ALBERT

KANN, RODOLPHE

KAY, ARTHUR

KENNARD, H. MARTYN

KENNEDY, C. S.

Kennedy, Sydney E.

Kenrick, Rt. Hon. William

Kitson, Sir James, Bart., M.P.

Knowles, James

Law, Ernest

Lawrence, Sir Trevor, Bart.

Leaf, Walter

Leatham, Arthur W.

Lessing, Prof. Dr. Julius, *Hon. Member*

Liddell, Adolphus G. C.

Lindsay, Leonard C.

Lippmann, Frederick, *Hon. Member*

Lloyd, R. Duppa

Lofft, Robert Emlyn

Loftie, Rev. W. J.

Loudon, Willoughby J. G.

Lucas, Arthur

Lyons, Lt.-Col. G. B. Croft

MacCallum, Andrew

Macdonald, J. Matheson

MacGregor, Rev. William

Mackenzie, Major-General Roderick

Mainwaring, Hon. W. F. B. Massey, M.P.

Malet, Colonel Harold

Marlay, Charles Brinsley

Marquand, H. G.

Marshall, Julian

PITT-RIVERS, LT.-GENERAL

PLUMBE, ROWLAND

POIX, EDMOND DE

PONSONBY, HON. GERALD H. B.

POYNTER, SIR EDWARD J., P.R.A.

PRICE, F. G. HILTON

PROPERT, J. LUMSDEN, M.D.

QUILTER, SIR WM. CUTHBERT, BART., M.P.

RADFORD, W. T., M.D.

RAPHAEL, LOUIS

RATE, LACHLAN MACKINTOSH

RATHBONE, W. G.

RAWLINSON, W. G.

REISS, FRITZ

REISS, JAMES

REISS, JAMES EDWARD

RIPON, MARQUIS OF, K.G.

ROBERTS, HUMPHREY

ROBINSON, C. NEWTON

ROBINSON, SIR J. CHARLES

ROGET, JOHN L.

ROME, W.

ROTHSCHILD, BARON EDMOND DE

RULAND, CHARLES, *Hon. Member*

SALTING, GEORGE

SALTMARSHE, ERNEST

SECKENDORFF, COUNT G. VON, *Hon. Member*

SEIDLITZ, DR. W. VON, *Hon Member.*

SEVERN, ARTHUR

SHATTOCK, T. FOSTER

SHERRIN, GEORGE

SICHEL, WALTER S.

SMITH, EDWARD

SMITH, T. VALENTINE

SMITH, WILLIAM

SOTHEBY, MAJOR-GENERAL, F. E.

SPALDING, SAMUEL

SPIELMANN, MARION H.

STAINTON, EVELYN

STANHOPE, HON. PHILIP, M.P.

STEPHENS, S. SANDERS

STIRLING-MAXWELL, SIR JOHN, BART., M.P.

STOKER, SIR W. THORNLEY

STRACHAN, GEORGE A.

STRONG, S. ARTHUR

SWINBURNE, C. A.

TAYLOR, JOHN EDWARD

TEBBS, H. VIRTUE, *Trustee*

TENNANT, SIR CHARLES, BART.

THEOBALD, H. STUDDY, Q.C.

THOMPSON, HENRY YATES

THOMPSON, SIR HENRY

TOMKINSON, MICHAEL

TOMS, T. H. L.

55

WILLIAMS, PETER
WILLIAMSON, GEORGE C.
WILSON, REV. HERBERT
WINDSOR, RT. HON. THE LORD
WITT, G. A.
WOERMANN, DR. KARL, *Hon. Member*
WORTHINGTON, THOMAS
WYNDHAM, GEORGE, M.P.
WYNDHAM, HON. PERCY
YATES, REV. S. A. THOMPSON

www.ingramcontent.com/pod-product-compliance
Lightning Source LLC
Chambersburg PA
CBHW030721110426
42739CB00030B/1064